KEEP THE
TASTE
OMELETS

Charlie Kridiotis

ALL THE FLAVOUR with fewer CALORIES and CARBS

Published by Kridio Publications
65 McNaughton Avenue
Wallaceburg, Ontario
N8A 1R7

Cover and food photography: Brent Foster
www.brentfosterphotography.com

Page 43: Robyn Mackenzie/Bigstock.com
Page 67: pilgrim.artworks/Bigstock.com

Design: Marcy Claman
Indexing: Heather Ebbs

First printing
Printed in Canada

Library and Archives Canada Cataloguing in Publication

Kridiotis, Charlie, 1985–

    Omelets : all the flavour with fewer calories and carbs / Charlie Kridiotis.

(Keep the taste)
Includes index.
ISBN 978-0-9880623-0-6

    1. Omelets. 2. Cooking (Eggs). 3. Low-fat diet—Recipes. I. Title.

TX745.K75 2012   641.6′75   C2012-903255-7

Callawind
Custom Cookbooks

Produced by Callawind Custom Cookbooks
(a division of Callawind Publications Inc.)
3551 St. Charles Boulevard, Suite 179
Kirkland, Quebec H9H 3C4
www.callawind.com

I would like to dedicate this book to the great town of Wallaceburg, Ontario. Thank you for all your help and local support through all my journeys.

Mom and Dad this would not be possible without the help and support I've received from you both; you have given me all the opportunities in life, making it possible to achieve my dreams.

CONTENTS

INTRODUCTION

I grew up in a small town in Ontario where mealtime meant meat and potatoes on almost every table. I have always had a love of food and craved more, which took me to London, Ontario, to expand my culinary skills. I studied at Fanshawe College in the Food and Beverage Program where I earned a Food and Beverage Management Diploma. I was then picked out of 500 students to attend the Concierge program (a post-diploma program). Most recently I acquired a Red Seal certification as a Chef. Earning my Red Seal required a lot of focus, discipline, and studying. This journey enabled me to expand my culinary skills and realize how important food and cooking are to me.

After moving back to my hometown, I purchased a restaurant and my love for food came back to haunt me, so to speak. I have always led an active lifestyle—playing many sports from soccer to hockey and almost everything in between. There has always been a need for me to be "fit," which is difficult when you own a restaurant and are surrounded by food every day. I love trying new recipes and I always try to watch what I eat, so I decided the best way to do both would be to take the flavours of my favourite foods—such as pizza or a simple sandwich— and prepare them with fewer calories and carbohydrates.

That is how I came up with the idea for a *Keep the Taste* cookbook series while eating healthier. In this edition I focus on omelets as an energy-filled, calorie-burning alternative to bread and carbohydrates. A study I came across recently compared an egg-based breakfast to a bagel-based breakfast, each containing the same number of calories. Those who ate eggs for breakfast consumed 163 fewer calories at lunch, felt less hungry, and ate 418 less calories over a 24-hour period.*

In this series of cookbooks I will suggest new ways to cook delicious foods with fewer calories and carbohydrates—all while keeping the taste!

* Layman, Donald K. "Protein Quantity and Quality at Levels above the RDA Improves Adult Weight Loss." *Journal of the American College of Nutrition:* J Am Coll Nutr December 2004 23: 631–636.

HOW TO PREPARE AN OMELET

There are a few different techniques for cooking an omelet but the same type of pan can be used for all recipes. You should always use a non-stick pan and either butter or vegetable oil to coat the bottom and sides, which will help prevent sticking. I suggest using a 6-inch pan. A larger pan will cause the omelet to spread and become too thin and dry. A smaller pan will make it difficult to cook the omelet all the way through and fold it. If you are preparing omelets for more than one person, it is best to cook them individually. All of the recipes in this book make 1 omelet.

When cooking omelets, always have all the ingredients prepared and out on the counter. It is important to have everything ready to be added to your omelet once the eggs have started cooking.

The most common type of omelet is a folded omelet. This method is very quick and versatile and can be useful when you are in a rush. Omelets should be prepared over medium-high heat. When the eggs begin to set, you can begin to lift the edges upward with a rubber spatula. This will ensure that the omelet does not stick and allows the uncooked eggs to run underneath. As you lift the edges, rotate the pan to prevent further sticking. At this time you can add different ingredients to personalize your creation. Once the bottom is set and golden brown, and the top is still a little moist, lift one edge and fold it over. Try not to break the omelet in half. Place the omelet on a plate, garnish, and serve immediately.

Achieving restaurant-style omelets requires a different technique—the one that is used in this book. Pan preparation is the same but an ovenproof metal handle is needed so the pan can be placed in the oven. This will help cook the top of the omelet without flipping it. As with the folded omelet, coat the pan with butter or vegetable oil to avoid sticking. A restaurant-style omelet is cooked on the stove for 2 to 3 minutes on medium. Once the bottom of the omelet is semi-set, lift the edges upward to prevent sticking, and add any further ingredients. Place the pan in the oven on the top rack, on the broil setting. Once the egg has set, remove the pan from the oven, fold the omelet in half with a rubber spatula, place on a plate, garnish, and serve immediately.

ABOUT EGGS

You know eggs contain protein but did you also know that they help control the rate your body absorbs calories? By staying full longer you eat less, which enables you to lose weight and have more energy. One large egg contains 5 grams of fat, only 70 calories, and 6 grams of protein, with just over half in the white and the remainder in the yolk.

In recent years further studies have been done on the benefits of eggs. The findings indicate consistently that eating eggs every day does not increase levels of "bad" cholesterol in the blood as was once believed.

A few facts about eggs:

» Eggs are versatile and can be used to add texture, structure, moisture, and nutrition while adding flavour to soups, sauces, and many other dishes.

» Eggs have a long fridge life of 4 to 5 weeks. If you are not sure an egg is fresh, you can easily test it by placing the egg in water. If the egg sinks, it is still fresh. If it floats, it is no longer Grade A fresh and should be discarded. This happens over time as the air cells in the egg expand, making the egg less dense and thus more buoyant.

» Egg whites whip better at room temperature. Eggs (whether raw or cooked) should not be kept at room temperature for more than 2 hours.

» Eggs can absorb odors and are best stored in a carton in the "core" of the refrigerator (not the door). Cracked or broken eggs should be discarded as they may contain bacteria.

» A cloudy egg white means that the eggs are extremely fresh.

» Double yolks and eggs that contain blood spots are safe to eat.

» If an egg is contaminated (from the hen), the bacteria will be in the yolk, which is why it is always important to fully cook eggs.

» There is no nutrition value difference between white eggs and brown eggs. White eggs come from white hens while brown eggs come from brown hens. Brown hens cost more to feed because they eat more—causing brown eggs to cost more at the grocery store.

RECIPES

Onion

3 large eggs

Salt and pepper to taste

¼ cup chopped white onion

¼ cup chopped green onion

2 slices cheddar cheese

2 onion rings

¼ cup ranch dressing

¼ cup onion strings

1. Preheat the broiler. Prepare an omelet pan (page 9).

2. Crack the eggs into a bowl, add salt and pepper, and mix well with a fork.

3. In the prepared pan, cook the white onion for 2 minutes on high heat. Add the eggs and reduce the heat to medium. Cook for 2 minutes. Place the green onion and cheddar cheese in the omelet.

4. Place the pan in the oven for 2 to 3 minutes to finish cooking.

5. Place the two onion rings on one half of the omelet, and fold the omelet onto a plate with a rubber spatula. Drizzle with the ranch dressing, top with the onion strings, and serve.

TIPS: The onion rings and strings can easily be made at home. Cut an onion into rings, and soak in seasoned milk or eggs. Season some flour with salt pepper, garlic powder and Cajun seasoning. Thoroughly coat the onion rings and deep fry at 375°F until golden brown. The strings are the same; just cut the rings in half.

Spinach and Feta

¼ cup fresh spinach

¼ cup butter

3 large eggs

1 tablespoon dried oregano

Pinch of salt and pepper

¼ cup crumbled feta cheese

1. Preheat the broiler. Prepare an omelet pan (page 9).

2. In a medium sauté pan, melt the butter on medium heat. Cook the spinach for about 5 minutes or until it wilts. Remove the spinach to a cutting board and chop.

3. Crack the eggs into a bowl, season with the salt, pepper, and oregano, and mix well with a fork.

4. In the prepared omelet pan, add the eggs and cooked spinach, reduce the heat to medium, and cook for 2 minutes. Add the feta cheese.

5. Place the pan in the oven for 2 to 3 minutes until the eggs are fully cooked and the feta is golden brown.

6. Fold the omelet in half with a rubber spatula, place on a plate, and serve.

Mushroom

¼ cup sliced button mushrooms

¼ cup sliced portabella mushrooms

¼ cup sliced shiitake mushrooms

¼ cup butter

Steak spice to taste

3 large eggs

1 tablespoon truffle oil*

Truffle oil is olive oil that has been infused with the earthy, deep flavour of the famous, expensive truffle mushroom.

1. Preheat the broiler. Prepare an omelet pan (page 9).

2. In a medium pan over high heat, sauté the mushrooms in butter and steak spice for 4 minutes.

3. Crack the eggs into a bowl, season with steak spice, and mix well with a fork.

4. In the prepared omelet pan over medium heat, add the mushroom mixture and eggs and cook for 2 minutes.

5. Place the pan in the oven for 2 to 3 minutes until the eggs are fully cooked.

6. Fold the omelet in half with a rubber spatula, place on a plate, drizzle with truffle oil, and serve.

Cordon Bleu

1 (5-ounce) boneless, skinless chicken breast, sliced into strips

Vegetable oil

3 large eggs

Cajun seasoning to taste

¼ cup diced cooked ham

2 slices Swiss cheese

1. Preheat the broiler. Prepare an omelet pan (page 9).

2. In a medium pan over medium heat, sauté the chicken in vegetable oil for about 5 minutes or until the chicken is cooked throughout. Set aside.

3. Crack the eggs into a bowl, add Cajun seasoning, and mix well with a fork.

4. In the prepared omelet pan over high heat, warm the ham and cooked chicken for 1 minute. Add the eggs, reduce the heat to medium, and cook for 2 minutes. Add the Swiss cheese.

5. Place the pan in the oven for 2 to 3 minutes until the eggs are fully cooked and the Swiss cheese has melted.

6. Fold the omelet in half with a rubber spatula, place on a plate, and serve.

Benedict

Hollandaise Sauce

3 egg yolks

3 tablespoons water

¾ cup clarified butter (see Tip below)

Omelet

3 strips Canadian bacon*

3 large eggs

Salt and pepper to taste

2 slices cheddar cheese

½ cup hollandaise sauce

1 parsley sprig, chopped

Also known as peameal bacon.

1. To make the sauce, in a small saucepan whisk the egg yolks and water over medium heat until the mixture falls in ribbons (ribbon-like strips will rest on top of the mixture). Remove from the heat. Slowly add the clarified butter, whisking constantly, until the sauce reaches a mayonnaise consistency. Set aside and keep warm.

2. Preheat the broiler. Prepare an omelet pan (page 9).

3. In the prepared omelet pan, sauté the bacon until cooked to 180°F, dice, and set aside.

4. Crack the eggs into a bowl, season with salt and pepper, and mix well with a fork.

5. Add the eggs, reduce the heat to medium, and cook for 2 minutes. Add the 2 slices of cheese.

6. Place the pan in the oven for 2 to 3 minutes until the eggs are fully cooked and the cheese has melted.

7. Fold the omelet in half with a rubber spatula, and place on a plate. Top with the hollandaise sauce, garnish with parsley, and serve.

TIP: To make clarified butter, melt butter over low heat. As the butter melts, a frothy film—consisting of milk fats and solids—develops. Using a tablespoon, remove all the fat and discard. What you have left is clarified butter.

Ham and Cheese

3 large eggs

Salt and pepper to taste

½ cup diced ham

2 slices cheddar cheese

1. Preheat the broiler. Prepare an omelet pan (page 9).

2. Crack the eggs into a bowl, add salt and pepper, and mix well with a fork.

3. In the prepared pan, add the ham and cook for 1 minute on high heat.

4. Add the eggs, reduce the heat to medium, and cook for 2 minutes. Add the cheese.

5. Place the pan in the oven for 2 to 3 minutes until the eggs are fully cooked and the cheese has melted.

6. Fold the omelet in half with a rubber spatula, place it on a plate, and serve.

Chili

There are many ways to make chili, so use your favourite recipe for this omelet. Whether you like it hot or mild, the choice is yours.

½ cup chili

3 eggs

1 tablespoon chili powder

¼ cup diced jalapeño

¼ cup grated cheddar and mozzarella cheese

¼ cup chopped green onion

1. Preheat the broiler. Prepare an omelet pan (page 9).

2. Heat the chili in a small saucepan over medium heat. Set aside.

3. Crack the eggs into a bowl, add the chili powder, and mix well with a fork.

4. In the prepared omelet pan, add the jalapeños and cook for 1 minute on high heat. Add the eggs, reduce the heat to medium, and cook for 2 minutes.

5. Place the pan in the oven for 2 to 3 minutes until the eggs are fully cooked.

6. Fold the omelet in half with a rubber spatula, then top with the chili and mixed cheese.

7. Return to the oven until the cheese has melted. Place the omelet on a plate, garnish with the green onion, and serve.

Cheddar

Cheddar Cheese Sauce (Yield: about 2 cups)

¼ cup butter

¼ cup diced garlic

¼ cup diced onion

¼ cup all-purpose flour

1½ cups 2% milk

1 cup shredded cheddar cheese

Omelet

3 large eggs

Salt and pepper to taste

2 slices cheddar cheese

1 slice applewood-smoked cheddar

¼ cup grated 3-year-old white cheddar

¼ cup cheddar cheese sauce

1. To make the sauce, in a small saucepan on medium heat, melt the butter. Sauté the garlic and onion for 2 minutes Add the flour, stir, then season with salt and pepper. Reduce the heat to low, and slowly add the milk and cheddar cheese. Continue to stir until the sauce is smooth and creamy.

2. Preheat the broiler. Prepare an omelet pan (page 9).

3. Crack the eggs into a bowl, season with salt and pepper, and mix well with a fork.

4. In the prepared pan, add the eggs and cook for 2 minutes over medium heat. Add all three types of cheddar cheese.

5. Place the pan in the oven for 2 to 3 minutes until the eggs are fully cooked and the cheese has melted.

6. Fold the omelet in half with a spatula, place on a plate, top with the cheddar cheese sauce, and serve.

Classic Salmon

Dill–Sour Cream Sauce (Yield: 1 cup)

1 cup low-fat sour cream

½ cup chopped dill

1 clove garlic, diced

Salt and pepper to taste

Omelet

1 (4-ounce) salmon fillet

3 large eggs

¼ cup chopped fresh dill

¼ cup capers

¼ cup diced onion

½ cup dill–sour cream sauce

1. To make the sauce, in a bowl, mix together the sour cream, dill, and garlic. Season with salt and pepper. Set aside in the refrigerator.

2. Preheat the broiler. Prepare an omelet pan (page 9).

3. Grill the salmon until cooked to 170°F. Chop, and set aside.

4. Crack the eggs into a bowl, add some dill and capers, and mix well with a fork (save some dill for the garnish).

5. In the prepared pan over high heat, add the cooked salmon and onion and cook for 2 minutes. Add the eggs, reduce the heat to medium, and cook for 2 minutes.

6. Place the pan in the oven for 2 to 3 minutes until the eggs are fully cooked.

7. Fold the omelet in half with a rubber spatula, place on a plate, and top with the dill–sour cream sauce. Garnish with fresh dill, and serve.

Blue Flame

Can't stand the heat? Don't eat this omelet!

½ cup lean ground beef

2 tablespoons Sriracha hot sauce*

3 large eggs

Pepper to taste

¼ cup diced jalapeños

¼ cup diced onion

2 slices Monterey Jack cheese

Also known as rooster sauce, a type of Thai hot sauce.

1. Preheat the broiler. Prepare an omelet pan (page 9).

2. Marinate the beef in 1 tablespoon of the hot sauce for at least 1 hour (the longer the better).

3. Cook the beef in a medium pan over medium heat until no longer pink. Drain the fat from the pan and set the beef aside.

4. Crack the eggs into a bowl, season with pepper and the remaining 1 tablespoon of hot sauce, and mix well with a fork.

5. In the prepared omelet pan, add the cooked beef, jalapeños, and onion and cook on high for 2 minutes. Add the eggs to the pan, reduce the heat to medium, and cook for 2 minutes. Add the Monterey Jack.

6. Place the pan in the oven for 2 to 3 minutes until the eggs are fully cooked and the cheese has melted.

7. Fold the omelet in half with a rubber spatula, place on a plate, and serve.

Mac and Cheese

Take your favourite macaroni and cheese recipe and add it to this omelet. Any leftover mac and cheese works very well here.

1 tablespoon butter

½ cup mac and cheese

3 large eggs

1 tablespoon paprika

¼ cup shredded cheddar and mozzarella cheese

1. Preheat the broiler. Prepare an omelet pan (page 9).

2. In a small pan over medium heat, melt the butter and heat the macaroni and cheese.

3. Crack the eggs into a bowl, add the paprika, and mix well with a fork.

4. In the prepared omelet pan, Add the eggs, reduce the heat to medium, and cook for 2 minutes. Add half the mac and cheese and the mixed cheese.

5. Place the pan in the oven for 2 to 3 minutes until the eggs are fully cooked.

6. Fold the omelet in half with a rubber spatula, place on a plate, top with the remaining mac and cheese, and serve.

Bloody Mary

Drink and *eat a Bloody Mary in the morning.*

Drink

¼ lime

Celery salt for rimmer

½ cup ice

1 ounce vodka

Dash of Worcestershire sauce

4 drops Tabasco sauce

1 teaspoon pickle juice

Salt and pepper to taste

1 celery stick

1 pickle spear

Omelet

3 large eggs

Salt and pepper to taste

Celery salt to taste

6 drops Tabasco

6 drops Worcestershire sauce

¼ cup chopped tomatoes

1 pickle spear

1. To make the drink, wet the rim of a glass with the lime and coat in the celery salt. Fill the glass with ice, and add the vodka, Tabasco, Worcestershire, and pickle juice. Season with salt and pepper. Garnish with the celery stick and pickle spear.

2. Preheat the broiler. Prepare an omelet pan (page 9).

3. Crack the eggs into a bowl, add the salt, pepper, celery salt, Tabasco, and Worcestershire, and mix well with a fork.

4. In the prepared pan over high heat, add the tomatoes and cook for 1 minute. Add the eggs, reduce the heat to medium, and cook for 2 minutes.

5. Place the pan in the oven for 2 to 3 minutes until the eggs are fully cooked.

6. Fold the omelet in half with a rubber spatula, and place on a plate. Garnish the omelet with the pickle spear, and serve.

Bruschetta

Bruschetta Mix (Yield: 2 cups)

1 cup diced tomatoes

¼ cup chopped basil

¼ cup diced red onion

1 tablespoon olive oil

¼ cup diced garlic

1 tablespoon balsamic vinegar

Juice of ½ lemon

Salt and pepper to taste

Omelet

3 large eggs

¼ cup balsamic vinaigrette

½ cup bruschetta mix

½ cup sliced bocconcini cheese

1. To make the bruschetta, in a bowl, combine all the ingredients and mix well. Set aside.

2. Preheat the broiler. Prepare an omelet pan (page 9).

3. Crack the eggs into a bowl, season with 1 tablespoon of the balsamic vinaigrette, and mix well with a fork.

4. In the prepared pan over high heat, cook the bruschetta mix for 2 minutes. Add the egg, reduce the heat to medium, and cook for 2 minutes. Add half the bocconcini slices .

5. Place the pan in the oven for 2 to 3 minutes until the eggs are fully cooked and the cheese has melted.

6. Fold the omelet in half with a rubber spatula, top with the remaining bruschetta mix and bocconcini, and return to oven to melt the cheese.

7. Place the omelet on a plate, drizzle with the remaining balsamic vinaigrette, and serve.

Mardi Gras

3 large eggs

1 tablespoon Cajun seasoning

¼ cup chopped onion

¼ cup chopped green pepper

¼ cup chopped celery

2 slices Monterey Jack cheese

¼ cup chipotle mayonnaise

1. Preheat the broiler. Prepare an omelet pan (page 9).

2. Crack the eggs into a bowl, add the Cajun seasoning, and mix well with a fork.

3. In the prepared pan over high heat, add the onion, green pepper, and celery, and sauté until the vegetables are fully cooked, about 3 minutes. Add the eggs, reduce the heat to medium, and cook for 2 minutes. Add the Monterey Jack.

4. Place the pan in the oven for 2 to 3 minutes until the eggs are fully cooked and the cheese has melted.

5. Fold the omelet in half with a rubber spatula, place on a plate, top with the chipotle mayonnaise, and serve.

Lobster

Compound Butter (Yield: 1 cup)

1 cup softened butter

¼ cup diced garlic

¼ cup chopped parsley

Salt and pepper to taste

Omelet

3 large eggs

Salt and pepper to taste

½ cup cooked lobster (or imitation lobster)

¼ cup crumbled goat cheese

¼ cup compound butter

¼ cup chopped parsley

1. To make the compound butter, combine the butter with the garlic and parsley. Mix well and season with salt and pepper. Cover with plastic wrap and roll into a tight tube. Place in the refrigerator until needed.

2. Preheat the broiler. Prepare an omelet pan (page 9).

3. Crack the eggs into a bowl, season with salt and pepper, and mix well with a fork.

4. In the prepared pan over high heat, add the lobster and cook for 2 minutes. Add the eggs, reduce the heat to medium, and cook for 2 minutes. Add the goat cheese.

5. Place the pan in the oven for 2 to 3 minutes until the eggs are fully cooked and the goat cheese has melted.

6. Fold the omelet in half with a rubber spatula. Cut a slice of the compound butter and place it on top of the omelet. Return the pan to the oven to melt the butter.

7. Place on a plate, garnish with the parsley, and serve.

Big Time Breakfast

3 large eggs

Pepper to taste

2 slices cooked bacon

2 cooked, chopped breakfast sausages

¼ cup cream cheese

1 cooked pancake

¼ cup melted butter

¼ cup maple syrup

1. Preheat the broiler. Prepare an omelet pan (page 9).

2. Crack the eggs into a bowl, season with pepper, and mix well with a fork.

3. In the prepared pan over high heat, add the bacon and sausage and cook for 1 minute. Add the eggs, reduce the heat to medium, and cook for 2 minutes. Add the cream cheese.

4. Place the pan in the oven for 2 to 3 minutes until the eggs are fully cooked and the cream cheese is warm.

5. Warm the pancake in the microwave for 45 seconds. Place it on a plate and spread with the butter.

6. Fold the omelet in half with a rubber spatula, place on top of the pancake, top with maple syrup, and serve.

Pierogi

1 large potato

3 large eggs

Salt and pepper to taste

¼ cup chopped white onion

2 strips chopped, cooked bacon

2 slices cheddar cheese

¼ cup sour cream

¼ cup chopped green onion

1. Preheat the broiler. Prepare an omelet pan (page 9).

2. Peel and cut the potato into cubes and parboil in a medium pot. Immediately cool the potato cubes in an ice bath, strain, and set aside.

3. Crack the eggs into a bowl, season with salt and pepper, and mix well with a fork.

4. In the prepared pan over high heat, add the potato and onion and cook for 4 minutes until golden brown. Add the bacon and cook for 1 minute. Add the eggs, reduce the heat to medium, and cook for 2 minutes. Add the cheddar cheese.

5. Place the pan in the oven for 2 to 3 minutes until the eggs are fully cooked and the cheese is melted.

6. Fold the omelet in half with a rubber spatula, and place on a plate. Top with the sour cream and green onion, and serve.

Goat Cheese-Pepper

½ cup crumbled goat cheese, at room temperature

½ cup diced roasted red peppers

4 tablespoons pepper

3 large eggs

1. Preheat the broiler. Prepare an omelet pan (page 9).

2. Mix together the goat cheese with ¼ cup of the roasted red peppers. Season with 2 tablespoons of the pepper, and mix well.

3. Crack the eggs into a bowl, season with the remaining 2 tablespoons pepper, and mix well with a fork.

4. In the prepared pan over high heat, cook the remaining ¼ cup red peppers for 1 minute. Add the eggs, reduce the heat to medium, and cook for 2 minutes. Add half of the goat cheese mixture.

5. Place the pan in the oven for 2 to 3 minutes until the eggs are fully cooked and the cheese has melted.

6. Fold the omelet in half, top with the remaining goat cheese mixture, and return to the oven until the goat cheese has melted. Place the omelet on a plate, and serve.

Rustic Parmesan

3 large eggs

1 tablespoon pesto

2 slices mozzarella cheese

½ cup tomato sauce

¼ cup shaved Parmesan cheese

1 fresh basil leaf

1. Preheat the broiler. Prepare an omelet pan (page 9).

2. Crack the eggs into a bowl, season with the pesto, and mix well with a fork.

3. In the prepared pan over high heat, add the eggs, reduce the heat to medium, and cook for 2 minutes. Add 2 slices of mozzarella cheese.

4. Place the pan in the oven for 2 to 3 minutes until the eggs are fully cooked and the cheese has melted.

5. Fold the omelet in half with a rubber spatula, and top with the tomato sauce and Parmesan cheese.

6. Return the pan to the oven until the cheese has melted. Place the omelet on a plate, garnish with the basil, and serve.

Mango-Cheddar

3 large eggs

1 tablespoon curry powder

¼ cup mango chutney

2 slices cheddar cheese

1. Preheat the broiler. Prepare an omelet pan (page 9).

2. Crack the eggs into a bowl, season with curry powder, and mix well with a fork.

3. In the prepared pan over high heat, add the mango chutney and cook for 1 minute. Add the eggs, reduce the heat to medium, and cook for 2 minutes. Add the cheddar cheese.

4. Place the pan in the oven for 2 to 3 minutes until the eggs are fully cooked and the cheddar has melted.

5. Fold the omelet in half with a rubber spatula, place on a plate, and serve.

Jalapeño Popper

Jalapeño-Cheddar Sauce (Yield: 3 cups)

¼ cup butter

¼ cup diced garlic

¼ cup diced onion

¼ cup diced jalapeño

¼ cup all-purpose flour

Salt and pepper to taste

1½ cups milk

1 cup shredded cheddar cheese

Omelet

¼ cup cream cheese, at room temperature

¼ cup diced jalapeño

3 large eggs

Salt and pepper to taste

2 slices cheddar cheese

½ cup jalapeño-cheddar sauce

1. To make the sauce, in a small saucepan heat the butter on medium heat. Sauté the garlic, onion, and jalapeño for 2 minutes. Stir in the flour and season with salt and pepper. Reduce the heat to low and slowly stir in the milk. Add the cheddar cheese and continue to stir until the sauce is smooth and creamy. Set aside and keep warm in a bowl placed over a pot of boiling water.

2. Preheat the broiler. Prepare an omelet pan (page 9).

3. Mix the cream cheese with half of the jalapeños.

4. Crack the eggs into a bowl, season with salt and pepper, and mix well with a fork.

5. In the prepared pan over high heat, cook the remaining jalapeños for 2 minutes. Add the eggs, reduce the heat to medium, and cook for 2 minutes. Add the cheddar cheese and the cream cheese mixture.

6. Place the pan in the oven for 2 to 3 minutes until the eggs are fully cooked and the cheese has melted.

7. Fold the omelet in half with a rubber spatula, and place on a plate. Top with the jalapeño-cheddar sauce, and serve.

Lemon-Pepper Goat Cheese

¼ cup crumbled pepper goat cheese

2 tablespoons pepper

3 large eggs

Pinch of salt

Juice of ½ lemon

¼ cup chopped onion

1. Preheat the broiler. Prepare an omelet pan (page 9).

2. Mix the goat cheese with 1 tablespoon of the pepper.

3. Crack the eggs into a bowl, season with the salt, remaining 1 tablespoon pepper, and lemon juice, and mix well with a fork.

4. In the prepared pan over high heat, add the onion and cook for 2 minutes. Add the eggs, reduce the heat to medium, and cook for 2 minutes. Add the goat cheese mixture.

5. Place the pan in the oven for 2 to 3 minutes until the eggs are fully cooked and the goat cheese has melted.

6. Fold the omelet in half with a rubber spatula, place on a plate, and serve.

Princess

4 ounces raw salmon

4 large egg whites (see Tip below)

¼ cup fresh chopped dill

¼ cup chopped tomatoes

¼ cup cooked chopped asparagus

1 clove garlic, diced

1. Preheat the broiler. Prepare an omelet pan (page 9).

2. Grill the salmon until cooked to 170°F. Chop and set aside.

3. Crack and separate the egg whites into a bowl, season with the dill, and mix well with a fork.

4. In the prepared pan over high heat, add the cooked salmon, tomatoes, and asparagus, and cook for 2 minutes. Add the egg whites, reduce the heat to medium, and cook for 2 minutes. Add the garlic.

5. Place the pan in the oven for 2 to 3 minutes until the eggs are fully cooked.

6. Fold the omelet in half with a rubber spatula, place on a plate, and serve.

TIP: The best way to separate the egg yolk from the egg white is by cracking the egg over a bowl and pouring the yolk back and forth between the shells. The egg white will fall into the bowl, leaving the yolk intact.

VARIATION: Mix together ¼ cup chopped dill and ½ cup low-fat sour cream. Season with salt and pepper. This simple dip is an excellent accompaniment to the omelet.

Dad's Jokes (CHEESY!)

Two ducks are sitting in a pond. One duck looks at the other and says, "Quack." The other duck looks at him confused and replies, "Hey that's what I was going to say!"

3 large eggs

¼ cup crumbled feta cheese

¼ cup crumbled goat cheese

Salt and pepper to taste

2 slices cheddar cheese

1 slice mozzarella cheese

½ cup cheddar cheese sauce (page 19)

1. Preheat the broiler. Prepare an omelet pan (page 9).

2. Crack the eggs into a bowl, add the feta cheese, goat cheese, and salt and pepper, and mix well with a fork.

3. In the prepared pan over high heat, add the eggs, reduce the heat to medium, and cook for 2 minutes. Add the cheddar and mozzarella cheese.

4. Place the pan in the oven for 2 to 3 minutes until the eggs are fully cooked and the cheese has melted.

5. Fold the omelet in half with a rubber spatula, place on a plate, and serve.

Philly Beef

3 large eggs

1 teaspoon steak spice

¼ cup chopped onion

¼ cup chopped pepper

4 slices roast beef

2 slices Swiss cheese

1. Preheat the broiler. Prepare an omelet pan (page 9).

2. Crack eggs into a bowl, add the steak spice, and mix well with a fork.

3. In the prepared pan over high heat, cook the onion and green peppers for 2 minutes. Add the eggs, reduce the heat to medium, and cook for 2 minutes. Add the roast beef and Swiss cheese.

4. Place the pan in the oven for 2 to 3 minutes until the eggs are fully cooked and the Swiss cheese has melted.

5. Fold the omelet in half with a rubber spatula, place on a plate, and serve.

Beef Taco

1 tablespoon hot sauce

1 tablespoon Tex-Mex seasoning

½ cup lean ground beef

¼ cup chopped onion

¼ cup chopped green pepper

3 large eggs

2 slices cheddar cheese

¼ cup shredded cheddar and mozzarella cheese

¼ cup shredded lettuce

¼ cup salsa

1. Mix together the hot sauce and ½ tablespoon of the Tex-Mex seasoning. Mix with the beef and marinate for at least an hour in the refrigerator.

2. Preheat the broiler. Prepare an omelet pan (page 9).

3. In a medium sauté pan over high heat, cook the beef for about 4 minutes or until no longer pink. Add the onion and green peppers and cook for another 3 minutes.

4. Crack the eggs into a bowl, add the remaining ½ tablespoon Tex-Mex seasoning, and mix well with a fork.

5. In the prepared omelet pan over medium heat, cook the eggs for 2 minutes. Add 1 slice of the cheddar cheese.

6. Place the pan in the oven for 2 to 3 minutes until the eggs are fully cooked and the cheese has melted.

7. Fold the omelet in half with a rubber spatula, top with the remaining slice of cheddar and the mixed cheese, then return to the oven until the cheese has melted.

8. Spread the lettuce over a plate and place the omelet on the lettuce. Top with the salsa, and serve.

Caesar

All the taste of a Caesar salad, but with the protein benefits of eggs.

3 large eggs

3 strips sliced cooked bacon

¼ cup chopped red onion

½ cup shaved Parmesan cheese

¼ cup Caesar dressing

1. Preheat the broiler. Prepare an omelet pan (page 9).

2. Crack the eggs into a bowl and mix well with a fork.

3. In the prepared pan over high heat, add the bacon and the red onion and cook for 1 minute. Add the eggs, reduce the heat to medium, and cook for 2 minutes. Add the Parmesan.

4. Place the pan in the oven for 2 to 3 minutes until the eggs are fully cooked and the cheese has melted.

5. Fold the omelet in half with a rubber spatula, place on a plate, top with the Caesar dressing, and serve.

Mediterranean

Tzatziki Sauce (Yield 1½ cups)

1 cup plain yogurt

½ cup peeled grated English cucumber

¼ cup chopped garlic

Pinch of salt and pepper

Omelet

3 large eggs

¼ cup sundried tomatoes

¼ cup chopped cooked spinach

¼ cup chopped red onion

¼ cup chopped garlic

¼ cup crumbled feta cheese

1 tablespoon dried oregano

½ cup tzatziki sauce

1. To make the sauce, strain the yogurt into a bowl. Squeeze the grated cucumber to remove any excess liquid. Mix together the cucumber with the yogurt and garlic and season with salt and pepper. Set aside.

2. Preheat the broiler. Prepare an omelet pan (page 9).

3. Crack the eggs into a bowl, season with the oregano, and mix well with a fork.

4. In the prepared pan over high heat, add the sundried tomatoes, spinach, and red onion and cook for 3 minutes. Add the eggs, reduce the heat to medium, and cook for 2 minutes. Add the garlic and feta.

5. Place the pan in the oven for 2 to 3 minutes until the eggs are fully cooked and the cheese has melted.

6. Fold the omelet in half with a rubber spatula, and place on a plate. Sprinkle the omelet with the oregano, and top with the tzatziki sauce.

Smoked Salmon

3 large eggs

1 tablespoon liquid smoke*

½ cup chopped cooked salmon

¼ cup chopped onion

2 slices smoked cheddar cheese

1 clove garlic, smoked and chopped**

Liquid smoke can be bought at the supermarket.

**You can substitute the smoked garlic with roasted garlic.*

1. Preheat the broiler. Prepare an omelet pan (page 9).

2. Crack the eggs into a bowl, add the liquid smoke, and mix well with a fork.

3. In the prepared pan over high heat, add the salmon and onion and cook for 2 minutes. Add the eggs, reduce the heat to medium, and cook for 2 minutes. Add the cheddar cheese and garlic.

4. Place the pan in the oven for 2 to 3 minutes until the eggs are fully cooked and the cheddar has melted.

5. Fold the omelet in half with a rubber spatula, place on a plate, and serve.

Bella Pizza

Bella Pizza is the pizza place my grandparents first opened when they moved to Canada. It is named after my amazing mother, so I named this omelet after her as well. Thanks Mom.

3 large eggs

1 tablespoon dried oregano

¼ cup chopped onion

¼ cup pepperoni

¼ cup chopped green pepper

¼ cup sliced mushrooms

¼ cup tomato sauce

2 slices mozzarella cheese

1. Preheat the broiler. Prepare an omelet pan (page).

2. Crack the eggs into a bowl, season with the oregano, and mix well with a fork.

3. In the prepared pan over high heat, cook the onion, pepperoni, green pepper, and mushrooms until the vegetables are fully cooked. Strain the grease from the pan if you wish. Add the eggs, reduce the heat to medium, and cook for 2 minutes.

4. Place the pan in the oven for 2 to 3 minutes until the eggs are fully cooked.

5. Fold the omelet in the pan with a rubber spatula, pour the tomato sauce over top, and add the cheese.

6. Return the pan to the oven to cook until the cheese has melted. Place the omelet on a plate, and serve.

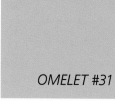

Gyro

3 large eggs

2 tablespoons dried oregano

½ cup cooked ground lamb

¼ cup chopped tomatoes

¼ cup chopped red onion

¼ cup chopped garlic

¼ cup crumbled feta cheese

½ cup tzatziki sauce (page 44)

1. Preheat the broiler. Prepare an omelet pan (page 9).

2. Crack the eggs into a bowl, season with 1 tablespoon of the oregano, and mix well with a fork.

3. In the prepared pan over high heat, add the lamb, tomatoes, and red onion, and cook for 3 minutes. Add the eggs, reduce the heat to medium, and cook for 2 minutes. Add the chopped garlic and feta.

4. Place the pan in the oven for 2 to 3 minutes until the eggs are fully cooked and the feta cheese has browned.

5. Fold the omelet in half with a rubber spatula, and place on a plate. Top with the remaining 1 tablespoon of oregano and tzatziki sauce.

Parm and Pepper Chicken, page 60

Pulled Pork

Pulled Pork

1 (4-pound) pork butt or shoulder

Salt and pepper to taste

¼ cup chili powder

¼ cup cumin

¼ cup garlic powder

¼ cup onion powder

Vegetable oil

1 cup root beer

1 cup BBQ sauce

Omelet

3 large eggs

Pinch of Cajun seasoning

½ cup pulled pork

¼ cup grated smoked cheddar cheese

¼ cup onion strings (page 12)

¼ cup BBQ sauce

1. To make the pork, preheat the oven to 250°F. Season the pork with salt, pepper, chili powder, cumin, garlic powder, and onion powder. Sear the pork in a roasting pan with vegetable oil and deglaze with root beer and your favourite BBQ sauce. Cook for 3 to 4 hours until the pork can be shredded with a fork. Shred all the meat with a fork, and cover with more BBQ sauce. Increase the oven heat to 350°F. Return the pork to the oven for 20 minutes to get a nice glaze on the top of the pork.

2. Preheat the broiler. Prepare an omelet pan (page 9).

3. Crack the eggs into a bowl, add the Cajun seasoning, and mix well with a fork.

4. In the prepared pan over high heat, add the pulled pork and cook for 1 minute. Add the eggs, reduce the heat to medium, and cook for 2 minutes. Add the cheddar cheese.

5. Place the pan in the oven for 2 to 3 minutes until the eggs are fully cooked and the cheese has melted.

6. Fold the omelet in half with a rubber spatula, and place on a plate. Top with the onion strings and BBQ sauce, and serve.

BLT

3 large eggs

Salt and pepper to taste

¼ cup diced tomatoes

2 strips sliced cooked bacon

1 lettuce leaf

1. Preheat the broiler. Prepare an omelet pan (page 9).

2. Crack the eggs into a bowl, season with salt and pepper, and mix well with a fork.

3. In the prepared pan over high heat, add the tomatoes and bacon and cook for 2 minutes. Add the eggs, reduce the heat to medium, and cook for 2 minutes.

4. Place the pan in the oven for 2 to 3 minutes until the eggs are fully cooked.

5. Place the lettuce leaf on a plate. Fold the omelet in half with a rubber spatula, place on top of the lettuce, and serve.

Oly the Greek

3 large eggs

2 tablespoons dried oregano

¼ cup bruschetta mix (page 26)

¼ cup cooked chopped spinach

¼ cup chopped red onion

¼ cup kalamata olives

¼ cup crumbled feta cheese

1. Preheat the broiler. Prepare an omelet pan (page 9).

2. Crack the eggs into a bowl, season with 1 tablespoon of the oregano, and mix well with a fork.

3. In the prepared pan over high heat, add the bruschetta mix, spinach, and red onion and cook for 3 minutes. Add the eggs, reduce the heat to medium, and cook for 2 minutes. Add the olives and feta.

4. Place the pan in the oven for 2 to 3 minutes until the eggs are fully cooked and the cheese has browned.

5. Fold the omelet in half with a rubber spatula place on a plate, top with remaining oregano, and serve.

Pepperoni

3 large eggs

Dried oregano to taste

¼ cup chopped onion

¼ cup sliced pepperoni

¼ cup tomato sauce

2 slices mozzarella cheese

4 whole pepperonis

1. Preheat the broiler. Prepare an omelet pan (page 9).

2. Crack the eggs into a bowl, season with the oregano, and mix well with a fork.

3. In the prepared pan over high heat, cook the onion and sliced pepperoni for 3 minutes. Strain the grease from the pan if you wish. Add the eggs, reduce the heat to medium, and cook for 2 minutes.

4. Place the pan in the oven for 2 to 3 minutes until the eggs are fully cooked.

5. Fold the omelet in half with a rubber spatula, pour the tomato sauce over top, and add the cheese. Place the 4 whole pepperonis over the cheese.

6. Return the pan to the oven until the cheese has melted. Place the omelet on a plate, and serve.

Italian

3 large eggs

¼ cup pesto

4 slices bocconcini cheese

5 slices cooked pancetta

¼ cup tomato sauce

¼ cup shaved Parmesan cheese

1 fresh basil leaf

1. Preheat the broiler. Prepare an omelet pan (page 9).

2. Crack the eggs into a bowl, add the pesto, and mix well with a fork.

3. In the prepared pan over medium heat, add the eggs and cook for 2 minutes. Add the bocconcini and 2 slices of the pancetta.

4. Place the pan in the oven for 2 to 3 minutes until the eggs are fully cooked and the cheese has melted.

5. Fold the omelet in half with a rubber spatula, and top with the remaining pancetta, tomato sauce, and Parmesan.

6. Return the pan to the oven to melt the cheese. Place the omelet on a plate, garnish with the basil, and serve.

Bacon-Cheddar Burger

2 strips bacon, cut into small pieces

½ cup lean ground beef

Salt and pepper to taste

¼ cup chopped onion

3 large eggs

2 slices cheddar cheese

1 lettuce leaf

3 tomato slices

3 red onion rings

1. Preheat the broiler. Prepare an omelet pan (page 9).

2. Cook the bacon in a sauté pan over medium heat. Remove the bacon from the pan, and reserve the fat.

3. Season the ground beef with salt and pepper.

4. In the prepared omelet pan over medium heat, cook the beef until it is no longer pink. Remove the beef from the pan, and keep warm.

5. Add the reserved bacon fat to the omelet pan with the beef fat. Add the onions and cook for 2 minutes on high heat, add the bacon and beef and cook for 1 minute.

6. Crack the eggs into a bowl, season with salt and pepper, and mix well with a fork.

7. Add the eggs, reduce the heat to medium, and cook for 2 minutes. Add the cheddar cheese.

8. Place the pan in the oven for 2 to 3 minutes until the eggs are fully cooked and the cheese has melted.

9. Fold the omelet in half with a rubber spatula, place on a plate over top of the lettuce leaf. Top with the red onion and tomato, and serve.

TIP: You can top your omelet with other burger condiments or even eat it in a hamburger bun.

Maple, Apple, and Pork

1 mild pork sausage

½ cup peeled diced apple

¼ cup butter

½ cup maple syrup

3 large eggs

Salt and pepper to taste

1. Preheat the broiler. Prepare an omelet pan (page 9).

2. Remove the casings from the pork sausage. Dice the sausage and sauté in a medium pan over medium heat; set aside.

3. In another small pan, sauté the apples with butter for 4 minutes on medium heat. Finish cooking the apples with half the maple syrup; set aside.

4. Crack the eggs into a bowl, add the salt, pepper, and remaining syrup, and mix well with a fork.

5. In the prepared omelet pan over high heat, add the cooked sausage and apples and reheat for 1 minute. Add the eggs, reduce the heat to medium, and cook for 2 minutes.

6. Place the pan in the oven for 2 to 3 minutes until the eggs are fully cooked. Fold the omelet in half with a rubber spatula, place on a plate, and serve.

Bolognese

½ cup ground beef

½ cup sliced mushrooms

¼ cup diced garlic cloves

½ cup tomato sauce

3 large eggs

¼ cup pesto

2 slices mozzarella cheese

¼ cup Parmesan cheese

1 fresh basil leaf

1. Preheat the broiler. Prepare an omelet pan (page 9).

2. In a medium sauté pan over medium heat, cook the ground beef. Midway through cooking, add half the mushrooms and garlic. When fully cooked, discard any extra grease and add the tomato sauce.

3. Crack the eggs into a bowl, add the pesto, and mix well with a fork.

4. In the prepared omelet pan over high heat, sauté the remaining mushrooms. Add the eggs, reduce the heat to medium, and cook for 2 minutes. Add the mozzarella cheese.

5. Place the pan in the oven for 2 to 3 minutes until the eggs are fully cooked and the cheese has melted.

6. Fold the omelet in half with a rubber spatula, top with the beef and tomato mixture (aka Bolognese sauce), and sprinkle with the Parmesan.

7. Return the pan to the oven and melt the cheese. Place the omelet on a plate, garnish with the basil, and serve.

Canadian

4 slices bacon, cut into small pieces

¼ cup maple syrup

3 large eggs

2 slices applewood-smoked cheddar

1. Preheat the broiler. Prepare an omelet pan (page 9).

2. In the prepared pan on medium heat, cook the bacon three-quarters of the way. Finish cooking the bacon with half the maple syrup.

3. Crack the eggs into a bowl, add the remaining maple syrup, and mix well with a fork. Add the eggs, reduce the heat to medium, and cook for 2 minutes. Add the cheese.

4. Place the pan in the oven for 2 to 3 minutes until the eggs are fully cooked and the cheese has melted.

5. Fold the omelet in half with a rubber spatula, place on a plate, and serve.

Parm and Pepper Chicken

3 large eggs

1 tablespoon pepper

½ cup cooked diced chicken

2 slices mozzarella cheese

¼ cup shredded Parmesan cheese

½ cup tomato sauce

½ cup pregrated Parmesan cheese

1. Preheat the broiler. Prepare an omelet pan (page 9).

2. Crack the eggs into a bowl, add the pepper, and mix well with a fork.

3. In the prepared pan over medium heat, cook the eggs for 2 minutes. Add the chicken, mozzarella cheese, and shredded Parmesan.

4. Place the pan in the oven for 2 to 3 minutes until the eggs are fully cooked and the mozzarella cheese has melted.

5. Fold the omelet in half with a rubber spatula, place on a plate, top with the tomato sauce and grated Parmesan, and serve.

Cheddar, page 19

Chicken Fajita

¼ cup hot sauce

¼ cup Tex-Mex seasoning

1 (4-ounce) boneless, skinless chicken breast, sliced into strips

3 large eggs

¼ cup chopped onion

¼ cup chopped red and green peppers

3 slices cheddar cheese

¼ cup shredded lettuce

¼ cup salsa

¼ cup sour cream

¼ cup chopped green onion

1. Preheat the broiler. Prepare an omelet pan (page 9).

2. Mix together the hot sauce and half the Tex-Mex seasoning. Marinate the chicken in the hot sauce mixture for 2 hours in the refrigerator.

3. In the prepared pan over medium heat, cook the chicken for 5 minutes.

4. Crack the eggs into a bowl, season with the remaining Tex-Mex seasoning, and mix well with a fork. Add the onion, and red and green peppers to the chicken in the pan, and cook for 3 minutes on high heat. Add the eggs, reduce the heat to medium, and cook for 2 minutes. Add 1 slice of cheddar cheese.

5. Place the pan in the oven for 2 to 3 minutes until the eggs are fully cooked and the cheese has melted.

6. Fold the omelet in half with a rubber spatula, and top with the remaining 2 slices of cheddar.

7. Return the pan to the oven and melt the cheese. Spread the lettuce on a plate and place the omelet over the lettuce. Top with the salsa, sour cream, and green onion, and serve.

Banana French Toast

3 large eggs

½ cup caramel sauce

1 banana, peeled and sliced

¼ cup whipped cream

1. Preheat the broiler. Prepare an omelet pan (page 9).

2. Crack the eggs into a bowl, add half the caramel sauce, and mix well with a fork.

3. In the prepared omelet pan over medium heat, add the eggs and cook for 2 minutes. Add the banana.

4. Place the pan in the oven for 2 to 3 minutes until the eggs are fully cooked.

5. Fold the omelet in half with a rubber spatula, and place on a plate. Drizzle with the remaining caramel sauce, top with the whipped cream, and serve.

Broccoli-Cheddar

Broccoli-Cheddar Sauce (Yield 3 cups)

¼ cup butter

¼ cup diced garlic

¼ cup diced onion

¼ cup cooked chopped broccoli

¼ cup all-purpose flour

Salt and pepper to taste

1½ cups 2% milk

1 cup shredded cheddar cheese

Omelet

½ cup cooked broccoli

3 large eggs

Salt and pepper to taste

2 slices cheddar cheese

¼ cup broccoli-cheddar sauce

1. To make the sauce, in a small saucepan over medium heat, melt the butter and sauté the garlic, onion, and cooked broccoli. Add the flour, stir, and season with salt and pepper. Reduce the heat to low and slowly stir in the milk and cheddar cheese. Continue to stir until the sauce is smooth and creamy. Set aside and keep warm.

2. Preheat the broiler. Prepare an omelet pan (page 9).

3. Crack the eggs into a bowl, season with salt and pepper, and mix well with a fork.

4. In the prepared pan over high heat, add the broccoli and reheat for 2 minutes. Add the eggs, reduce the heat to medium, and cook for 2 minutes. Add the cheddar cheese.

5. Place the pan in the oven for 2 to 3 minutes until the eggs are fully cooked and the cheese has melted.

6. Fold the omelet in half with a rubber spatula, place on a plate, top with the broccoli-cheddar sauce, and serve.

Pig

2 slices bacon

2 slices pancetta

2 slices prosciutto

1 mild sausage

1 slice Canadian bacon

4 large eggs

¼ cup diced cooked ham

2 slices cheddar cheese

1. Preheat the broiler. Prepare an omelet pan (page 9).

2. In a medium sauté pan, cook the bacon, pancetta, and prosciutto. Reserve the fat and set aside.

3. Remove the sausage casing and fry in the bacon fat. Chop and set aside.

4. Grill the bacon, dice, and set aside.

5. Crack the eggs into a bowl and mix well with a fork.

6. In the prepared omelet pan on high heat, add the cooked bacon, pancetta, prosciutto, sausage, bacon, and ham, and cook for 1 minute. Add the eggs, reduce the heat to medium, and cook for 3 minutes. Add the cheddar cheese.

7. Place the pan in the oven for 2 to 4 minutes until the eggs are fully cooked and the cheese has melted.

8. Fold the omelet in half with a rubber spatula, place on a plate, and serve.

Ultimate Western

2 slices Canadian bacon

4 large eggs

½ cup chopped red and green peppers

¼ cup grated sharp cheddar cheese

1. Preheat the broiler. Prepare an omelet pan (page 9).

2. Grill the bacon, reserving the fat. Chop the bacon into bite-sized pieces, and set aside.

3. Crack the eggs into a bowl and mix well with a fork.

4. In the prepared pan over high heat, add the reserved bacon fat. Add the cooked bacon, peppers, and onion, and cook for 3 minutes. Add the eggs, reduce the heat to medium, and cook for 2 minutes. Add the cheddar cheese.

5. Place the pan in the oven for 2 to 3 minutes until the eggs are fully cooked and the cheese has melted.

6. Fold the omelet in half with a rubber spatula, place on a plate, and serve.

Beef-Jalapeño

3 large eggs

Salt and pepper to taste

¼ cup diced jalapeños

½ cup cooked ground beef

2 slices cheddar cheese

¼ cup jalapeño-cheddar sauce (page 34)

¼ cup chopped green onion

1. Preheat the broiler. Prepare an omelet pan (page 9).

2. Crack the eggs into a bowl, season with salt and pepper, and mix well with a fork.

3. In the prepared pan over high heat, add the jalapeños and ground beef, and cook for 2 minutes. Add the eggs to the pan, reduce the heat to medium, and cook for 2 minutes. Add the cheddar cheese.

4. Place the pan in the oven for 2 to 3 minutes until the eggs are fully cooked and the cheese has melted.

5. Fold the omelet in half with a rubber spatula, and place on a plate. Top with the jalapeño-cheddar cheese sauce, and garnish with the green onion.

Buffalo Chicken

Vegetable oil

1 (5-ounce) boneless, skinless chicken breast, sliced into strips

¼ cup hot sauce

3 large eggs

¼ cup crumbled blue cheese

¼ cup ranch dressing

2 carrot sticks

2 celery sticks

1. Preheat the broiler. Prepare an omelet pan (page 9).

2. In a medium sauté pan, add some vegetable oil and cook the chicken for about 7 to 10 minutes. Remove the chicken from the pan and add half the hot sauce.

3. Crack the eggs into a bowl, add the remaining hot sauce, and mix well with a fork.

4. In the prepared pan over high heat, add the eggs, reduce the heat to medium, and cook for 2 minutes. Add the chicken and blue cheese.

5. Place the pan in the oven for 2 to 3 minutes until the eggs are fully cooked and the cheese has melted.

6. Fold the omelet in half with a rubber spatula, and place on a plate. Top with the ranch dressing, and garnish with the carrot and celery sticks.

Apple-Cinnamon

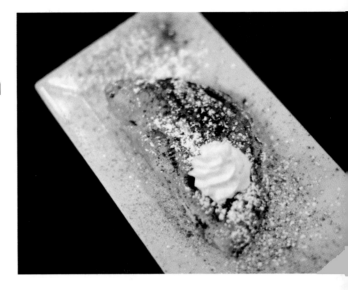

8 peeled green apple slices

¼ cup maple syrup

4 large egg whites

1 tablespoon ground cinnamon

¼ teaspoon vanilla extract

¼ cup icing sugar

¼ cup whipped cream

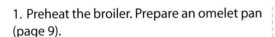

1. Preheat the broiler. Prepare an omelet pan (page 9).

2. Sauté the apples in maple syrup until caramelized. Cool, and set aside.

3. Crack the eggs and separate the whites into a bowl. Add the cinnamon and vanilla extract, and mix well with a fork.

4. In the prepared pan over high heat, add the apples and reheat for 2 minutes. Add the eggs, reduce the heat to medium, and cook for 2 minutes.

5. Place the pan in the oven for 2 to 3 minutes until the eggs are fully cooked.

6. Fold the omelet in half with a rubber spatula, and place on a plate. Top with the cinnamon, icing sugar, and whipped cream, and serve.

TIPS: You can also make this omelet with whole eggs. Use 3 whole eggs instead of 4 whites. To separate eggs, see the tip on page 37.

Strawberry and Chocolate

½ cup strawberries

½ cup maple syrup

4 large egg whites

1 tablespoon cocoa powder

¼ teaspoon vanilla extract

½ cup strawberry cream cheese

¼ cup chocolate sauce

½ cup whipped cream

1. Preheat the broiler. Prepare an omelet pan (page 9).

2. Cut the strawberries into quarters. In a small pan over medium-high heat, sauté the strawberries in the maple syrup until caramelized. Cool, and set aside.

3. Crack the eggs and separate the whites into a bowl. Add ½ tablespoon of the cocoa powder and the vanilla extract, and mix well with a fork until the cocoa powder is completely incorporated.

4. In the prepared omelet pan over high heat, add half the strawberries and cook for 2 minutes. Add the eggs, reduce the heat to medium, and cook for 2 minutes. Add the cream cheese.

5. Place the pan in the oven for 2 to 3 minutes until the eggs are fully cooked and the cream cheese has melted.

6. Fold the omelet in half with a rubber spatula, and place on a plate. Top with the remaining strawberries, the chocolate sauce, and whipped cream, and serve.

TIPS: You can also make this omelet with whole eggs. Use 3 whole eggs instead of 4 whites. To separate eggs, see the tip on page 37.

INDEX TO OMELET INGREDIENTS

ham, *continued*
    with chicken and Swiss cheese, 15
hollandaise sauce, 16

I
Italian omelet, 55

J
jalapeño-cheddar sauce, 34
jalapeño peppers
    with beef and cheddar, 68
    with cheddar, 34

L
lamb, ground, with vegetables, feta, and
    tzatziki, 48
lemon, with pepper goat cheese, 36
lobster, with goat cheese and garlic butter,
    28

M
Mac and Cheese omelet, 23
macaroni, with cheeses, 23
mango chutney, with cheddar, 33
maple syrup
    with apples and cinnamon, 71
    with apples and pork sausage, 57
    with bacon and cheddar, 59
    with strawberries and chocolate sauce, 73
Mardi Gras omelet, 27
Mediterranean omelet, 44
Monterey Jack cheese
    in Cajun omelet, 27
    with ground beef and hot sauce, 22
mozzarella cheese
    with Bolognese sauce, 58

mozzarella cheese, *continued*
    with chicken, pepper, and Parmesan,
      60
    in chili, 18
    with ground beef and Tex-Mex
      seasonings, 40
    with Parmesan, pesto, and tomato sauce,
      32
    with pepperoni, onions, and tomato
      sauce, 54
    in pepperoni pizza omelet, 47
    with three other cheeses, 38
mushrooms, 14
    with ground beef, tomato sauce, pesto,
      and cheeses, 58
    with pepperoni, onions, peppers, cheese,
      and tomato sauce, 47

O
olives, with spinach, onions, and feta, 53
Oly the Greek omelet, 53
onions
    with cheese, 12
    with pepperoni, pepper, mushrooms,
      cheese, and tomato sauce, 47
    with pepperoni, tomato sauce, and
      mozzarella, 54
    with peppers, celery, and cheese, 27
    with potatoes, bacon, cheddar, and sour
      cream, 30
    with spinach, olives, and feta, 53
    with sundried tomatoes, spinach, garlic,
      and feta, 44

P
pancakes, with bacon and sausage, 29

SPECIAL THANKS

A special thanks to the following people who helped make this book possible:

Oly Kridiotis

Leyea Kridiotis

Constance Kridiotis

Brent Foster Photography
www.brentfosterphotography.com

Stacey Falconer

Daniel Whitlock

Justin McNeil

Rod Langstaff

Christina McFadden

Tayler Gallerno

Ashley Myers

The staff of Crabby Joe's Wallaceburg

The great town of Wallaceburg